Serve Meals that are Creative, Easy, and Nutritious
—Collect the Entire Series

Healthy & Delicious

Healthy Cooking on the Run
Healthy Snacks for Kids
Creative Soups & Salads
Quick & Easy Pasta Recipes

New Ways to Enjoy Chicken
Favorite Seafood Recipes
No Salt, No Sugar, No Fat
Fresh Vegetable Cookbook

Gourmet Product Tie-Ins

The Wok
Wok Appetizers & Light Snacks
Quiche & Souffle
Easy Microwave Cooking

Crepes & Omelets
Food Processor
Fondue
Extra Special Crockery Pot Recipes

Entertaining Made Easy

Cooking for 1 or 2
Brunch
Cocktails & Hors d'Oeuvres
Bread Baking

Cookies
Authentic Mexican Cooking
Fisherman's Wharf
Kid's Cookbook

Who Do You Know That Could Use One Of These Popular Titles?

Nitty Gritty Cookbooks are available at better gourmet, department and book stores. If you have difficulty finding them, write to Nitty Gritty at the address below and ask us about our special offer for orders of 4 books or more. Buy a few extra copies for those special gifts this year. "Offer subject to change without notice."

nitty gritty cookbooks P.O. Box 2008-BC, Benicia, CA 94510

Holiday
COOKBOOK

Edited by Maureen Reynolds

Illustrated by Dorothy Cutright Davis

A Nitty Gritty Book*
Published by
Nitty Gritty Productions
P.O. Box 2008
Benicia, California 94510

*Nitty Gritty Books-Trademark
Owned by Nitty Gritty Productions
Benicia, California

Printed in the U.S.A.
by Mariposa Press
Benicia, California

ISBN 0-911954-64-3
Library of Congress Catalog Card Number 81-83232

Table of Contents

A Fall Breakfast For Family or Friends

To pique your appetite for this hearty meal, take a brisk morning walk. The cool air and the crunch of autumn leaves 'neath your feet are the perfect prelude to this Fall Breakfast.

To spruce up your table, how about a centerpiece? A pumpkin, carved or uncarved is inexpensive and attractive. Place it on a bed of straw and add a few dried flowers. A basket brimful of lacquered squash is also pretty. A fresh bouquet of autumn-colored mums or lillies is a traditional favorite.

For perfect link sausage, prepare them according to these instructions: prick each sausage four or five times with a fork. Place in a skillet and cover with water. Heat to a gentle simmer. Poach for 15 to 20 minutes, or until thoroughly cooked. Drain and cool. Refrigerate for up to 2 days prior to serving. When ready to serve, lightly butter a skillet. Cook sausages in a skillet over medium heat until golden brown and piping hot. Serve immediately on a warmed platter.

Menu

Cocoa Mocha
Perfect Omelets
Corn Fritters with Maple Syrup
Link Sausages (see introduction)
Baked Apples with Cream
orange juice
Serves 6

Cocoa Mocha

This mix keeps for up to one week in the refrigerator.

1 can (15 ozs.) sweetened condensed milk
1 bar (4 ozs.) German sweet chocolate, melted
1 cup whipping cream, whipped

Melt chocolate with condensed milk in the top of a double boiler over low heat. Stir occasionally. Cool. Fold whipped cream into cooled chocolate mixture.

To serve: put 1/4 cup of mixture into a mug. Fill to the top with hot coffee. Stir and serve. Store any remaining mixure covered in the refrigerator. Makes enough for 6 people to have two servings each.

From Brunch

Perfect Omelets

If followed carefully, this recipe will yield perfect omelets, even if you've never cooked them before. For really hearty appetites, make the 3-egg omelet. Mix the ingredients for each omelet separately.

2-egg omelet:
2 eggs
2 tsp. water
dash salt
2 drops Tabasco sauce
1 tbs. butter

3-egg omelet:
3 eggs
3 tsp. water
dash salt
3 drops Tabasco sauce
1-1/2 tbs. butter

Read the complete recipe and directions before starting to cook. Gather all ingredients and equipment before starting to cook. Break eggs into a small bowl. Add water, salt and Tabasco sauce. Beat with a fork until whites and yolks are just blended, about 50 strokes or 20 seconds. Eggs should not foam. Put butter into a well-seasoned omelet pan or skillet. Place pan over moderately high heat. Rotate pan to distribute butter. When butter has stopped foaming, but before it has browned, pour eggs into pan. Allow eggs to set for a few seconds before starting to stir them. Make circular movements around the bottom of the pan with the

flat side of a fork, lifting the cooked egg up as you stir. When omelet has set on the bottom, tilt the pan and lift the edge of the omelet to allow any uncooked egg on top to flow under cooked portion. Shake pan vigorously to loosen omelet and prevent it from sticking. Smooth the top of the omelet with the fork. Cook a few seconds more. An omelet should be only slightly brown on the outside and still creamy, but not liquid on the inside. Fold omelet into thirds by turning the edge opposite the handle onto the center. Then fold the edge near the handle over the middle. Grasp the handle of the pan in your upturned palm. Roll omelet out onto a warm plate, seam side down. Brush with melted butter for a nice sheen. Serve each person immediately, or keep each omelet warm in a 200°F. oven until you've made all the omelets.

From Crepes and Omelets

Corn Fritters

Serve these crispy fritters with lots of heated maple syrup.

2 eggs, separated (at room temperature)
1 cup all-purpose flour
2 tsp. baking powder
1 can (15 ozs.) creamed corn
1/4 cup sugar
powdered sugar

Beat egg whites until stiff using an electric mixer. Place egg yolks in a separate bowl, beat slightly. Sift flour and baking powder into yolks and stir. Add creamed corn and sugar to egg yolk mixture, combining well. Fold in egg whites. Pour vegetable oil into a skillet to a depth of 1/2 inch. Heat oil to 375°F. Drop fritters by spoonfuls into hot oil. Don't crowd skillet. Cook until golden, turning once. Drain on paper towels. Sprinkle with powdered sugar. Keep warm in 200°F. oven while preparing the rest. Makes about 30 fritters.

From Brunch

Baked Apples with Cream

These are delicious warm or cold. Serve them for dessert as well as breakfast.

6 baking apples, cored, not peeled (Granny Smith or Golden Delicious)
1/3 cup firmly packed brown sugar
3 tbs. chopped walnuts
1/3 cup chopped dates or raisins
2 tsp. or more cinnamon
1/3 cup butter, in small bits
2 cups heavy cream

Wash apples. Arrange in baking dish. Combine brown sugar, walnuts and dates. Divide mixture among apples and stuff cores. Sprinkle with cinnamon and dot with butter. Add water to 1/4-inch deep to baking pan.* Bake in 350°F. oven for 45 minutes, or until tender when pierced with a fork. Serve with cream. Makes 6 servings.
*May be made up to 1 day ahead to this point.

A Trim-the-Tree Brunch

Whether the Christmas tree you're planning is large or small; real or artificial, this tasty meal is reason enough to plan a Trim-the-Tree Brunch. This is also a suitable brunch for house guests during the Yuletide season or a football watcher's party.

The Champagne Mimosa is a wonderful "eye-opener." If you really want to make points with your guests, hand them a glass filled with this delicious concoction as you greet them at the door. To make them, simply fill wine or champagne glasses with equal parts of orange juice (preferably fresh) and champagne.

To vary this menu, try some of these alternatives: substitute Cherry Cream Cheese Spread (page 48) for the Brandied Camembert; and/or substitute Bourbon Bread (page 53) for the Pumpkin Muffins; and/or substitute Cookie Jewels (page 54) for the Christmas Butter Wreaths.

9

Menu

Champagne Mimosa (see introduction)
Brandied Camembert
Hot Buttered Cranberry Punch
Fantastic Mushroom Eggs with Cheese and Cream Sauce
Sausage Ring
Pumpkin Muffins
Christmas Butter Wreaths
coffee, tea
Serves 8 to 10

Brandied Camembert

This very elegant appetizer should be prepared at least 24 hours in advance to allow the flavors to mellow. Serve with very plain crackers or wedges of unpeeled fresh apples or pears. If you want to slice the apples or pears in advance, sprinkle each slice with a little fresh lemon juice. Store in plastic wrap up to 6 hours.

This can also be served as a European-style dessert, and Brandied Camembert makes a nice gift from your kitchen around holiday time.

2 pkgs. (8 ozs. each) Camembert cheese
1 cup butter

1/4 cup brandy
1 cup sliced almonds, toasted (see page 48)

Remove rind from Camembert and discard. Cut cheese and butter into 1-inch cubes. Using a food processor or electric mixer, combine Camembert, butter and brandy until thoroughly blended. Divide mixture in half. Shape each half into a ball, using plastic wrap (this will keep fingers from sticking). Press toasted almonds over the surface. Wrap tightly and refrigerate. Remove from the refrigerator 20 minutes before serving. Makes 2 cheese balls.

Hot Buttered Cranberry Punch

1 can (16 ozs.) jellied cranberry sauce
1/3 cup firmly packed brown sugar
1/4 tsp. cinnamon
1/4 tsp. alspice
1/8 tsp. cloves
1/8 tsp. nutmeg
1/8 tsp. salt
2 cups water
2 cups unsweetened pineapple juice
butter pats, for serving

Combine all ingredients except butter pats in a large saucepan. Stir over medium heat until cranberry sauce is melted. Reduce heat to simmer and cook gently for 2 hours. To serve, ladle into mugs and float a pat of butter on top of each. Serves 8 to 10.

From Brunch

Sausage Ring

This very simple idea glorifies store bought sausage. Garnish your Sausage Ring with lots of fresh parsley sprigs and you have a feast for the eyes as well as the palate.

3 pkgs. (16 ozs. 3 each) ground pork sausage
parsley sprigs

Press sausage firmly into a 9-inch ring mold. Bake at 350°F. for 45 minutes to 1 hour, or until pork is thoroughly cooked. Drain fat. Unmold sausage onto a heated serving plate. Garnish with parsley sprigs. Serves 8 to 10.

From Brunch

Fantastic Mushroom Eggs
with Cheese and Cream Sauce

This rich casserole can be made up to two days before you plan to serve it. Simply refrigerate it after you finish sprinkling it with the cheeses. Bake it for 20 to 30 minutes at 350°F. and broil it briefly, if desired.

For the mushrooms:
2 tbs. butter
1 lb. fresh mushrooms, thinly sliced
salt, pepper—a dash each

For the eggs:
1 dozen eggs
1/2 cup butter

Melt 2 tablespoons of butter in a large skillet over medium heat. Saute mushrooms until soft. Sprinkle with salt and pepper. Set aside. Break eggs into a large bowl and whisk thoroughly. Add salt and pepper. Melt half of the 1/2 cup butter in a large skillet over very low heat. Pour eggs into skillet. Gently scramble eggs. When eggs have turned into very soft curds, stir in remaining butter and sprinkle with salt and pepper. Set aside. Make a cream sauce and shred the cheeses:

Sauce:
6 tbs. butter
6 tbs. all-purpose flour
1 pint half-and-half

Cheeses:
4 ozs. Parmesan cheese, grated
4 ozs. Swiss or Gruyere cheese, grated
4 ozs. Cheddar cheese, grated
salt, pepper—a dash each

Melt butter in a saucepan over medium-low heat. Stir in flour. Allow mixture to bubble for 30 seconds. Add salt and pepper. Stir in cream. Whisk over low heat until mixture thickens. Meanwhile, grate cheeses.

To Assemble:

Lightly butter the bottom of a large ovenproof casserole. Sprinkle with half of the Parmesan. Spread a thin layer of the cream sauce over cheese. Place half of the scrambled eggs on top. Add half of the remaining cream sauce to mushrooms, stir. Place mushroom mixture on top of the eggs. Sprinkle with half of the grated Swiss and Cheddar. Add rest of eggs. Top with remaining cream sauce. Sprinkle with remaining Swiss, Cheddar and Parmesan. Broil 6 inches from the heat until cheese is bubbly and eggs are heated through. Serves 8 to 10.

Pumpkin Raisin Muffins

If you like, sprinkle the tops of these muffins with the Crunchy Nut Topping.

2 eggs
1 cup milk
1 cup canned pumpkin
1/2 cup melted butter
1 cup sugar
3 cups all-purpose flour
4 tsp. baking powder

1 tsp. salt
1 tsp. EACH cinnamon and nutmeg
1 cup raisins
Nut Crunch Topping (optional):
   2/3 cup firmly packed brown sugar
   2/3 cup chopped walnuts
   1 tsp. cinnamon

Combine eggs, milk, pumpkin, butter and sugar in a medium-sized bowl. Stir until blended. Sift flour, baking powder, salt and 1 teaspoon each of cinnamon and nutmeg into pumpkin mixture. Stir until just moistened. Batter should be lumpy. Fold in raisins. Fill greased muffin cups about two thirds full. Combine Nut Crunch Topping ingredients in a small bowl. Sprinkle evenly over tops of muffins. Bake at 400°F. for 18 to 20 minutes. Serve hot. Makes 24 muffins.

From Brunch

Christmas Butter Wreaths (Berliner Kranzer)

Sometimes this favorite Scandinavian cookie is adorned with candied cherry bits and chopped pistachios for extra holiday spirit. For variety twist strips of dough into pretzel shapes instead of rings.

1 cup butter (at room temperature)
1/2 cup sugar
2 raw egg yolks
2 hard-cooked egg yolks, sieved
1/2 tsp. almond extract
2-1/2 cups all-purpose flour

Topping:
1 egg white
1 tbs. water
1/2 cup finely chopped blanched almonds
2 tbs. sugar

Beat butter and 1/2 cup sugar together until creamy. Stir in raw and hard-cooked egg yolks and almond extract. Add flour and mix until smoothly blended. Pinch off small bits of dough and roll each into a strip 4 inches long. Bring ends together, pinching to make a ring. Place on greased baking sheets. Beat egg white and water together until frothy and brush on cookies. Sprinkle with almonds and sugar. Bake in a 375°F. oven for 10 minutes, or until golden brown. Remove to wire racks immediately and let cool. Makes 2 dozen.

From Cookies

A Traditional Thanksgiving or Christmas Dinner

The holidays are a magical time, full of joy and anticipation. Often, though, there doesn't seem to be enough time to enjoy family or friends. And, if you work full time, holiday entertaining can be an exhausting struggle. The menu in this chapter contains traditional and updated favorites, all created for their ease of preparation. Many can be prepared either partially or completely in advance. The following "plan of action" organizes your cooking schedule for you. This will help insure the success of your meal and allow you to remain "cool and collected."

TWO DAYS BEFORE
- Buy all ingredients, including wine and cordials.
- Store defrosted turkey in refrigerator.
- Make Cranberry Relish. Cover and store in refrigerator.
- Make Yams up to point of baking them in oven. Refrigerate covered casserole.

DAY BEFORE
- Make pastry for pumpkin pie. Wrap in plastic wrap and refrigerate.
- Saute onions for Green Beans Lyonnaise. Cover and refrigerate. Cut up green beans. Store in plastic bag in refrigerator.
- Bake cornbread and biscuits for stuffing. Cover tightly and store at room temperature. Dice celery and onions for stuffing. Store separately in plastic bags in refrigerator.
- Remove giblets from turkey and simmer in 2 to 3 quarts of salted water until tender, about 2 hours. Cool. Finely chop enough for gravy. Store, covered, in refrigerator.
- Make Ambrosia. Cover and refrigerate.

DAY OF DINNER

- 7 hours before dinner, bake pie. Let rest at room temperature. Whip cream for topping, if desired.
- While pie is baking, finish stuffing for turkey. Stuff turkey just before roasting it.
- 5 or more hours before dinner, roast turkey. When done, let rest at room temperature 15 minutes before carving and unstuffing.
- While turkey is cooking, prepare gravy and let rest at room temperature. Reheat before serving.
- Peel potatoes and cover them with salted water in a large saucepan or Dutch oven. 45 minutes before turkey is done, cook them. Mash when tender, adding lots of butter, milk, salt and white pepper to taste. Cover to keep warm until serving.
- When turkey comes out of oven, cook yams.
- 15 minutes before dinner, steam green beans until just tender. Add onions and seasonings and toss over medium-high heat until piping.

Menu

Ambrosia
Roast Turkey with Cornbread Stuffing
Mashed Potatoes*, Giblet Gravy
Fresh Cranberry Relish
Yams with Rum and Walnuts
Green Beans Lyonnaise
Pumpkin Pie with Perfect Crust
Fruitcake
coffee, tea, wine, cordials
Serves 12 to 16

*recipe not included

Ambrosia

Serve in your prettiest compote dish.

6 oranges
2 Golden Delicious apples
2 cups sugar
1-1/2 cups pineapple chunks
1 cup coconut (moist flakes)
1 cup broken walnuts

Cut away the peeling on the oranges. Cut flesh into bite size chunks. Peel, core and chop the apples. Quickly toss all the ingredients together.

Store in the refrigerator in a covered container for at least 24 hours—longer if you like.

Do not make a substitution for the walnuts, this recipe gets its flavor from these nuts.

Roast Turkey

A dry white wine, such as Chardonnay, Chablis, Sauvignon Blanc or Gewurtztraminer make a nice accompaniment to turkey.

A 16 to 20 lb. hen turkey should serve 12 to 16 nicely. Since cooking time varies with each bird, follow the chart on the wrapper, allowing 1 hour more. This will give a time for further cooking, if needed, and a period for the bird to rest after cooking.

To prepare the bird, remove the giblets and neck from inside. Set them aside for the gravy. Rinse the turkey, inside and out with water. Pat dry with paper towels. Rub inside with salt and pepper. Brush a generous quantity of melted butter on the outside of the turkey. Sprinkle with salt and pepper. Stuff turkey. Truss. Place bird in a baking pan. Cover the entire bird with a tent of aluminum foil. Roast. Remove this tent to baste every half hour or so, and remove it entirely near the end of the cooking time if additional browning is needed. To test for doneness, pierce bird deeply in thigh area. If liquid runs clear or slightly yellow-colored, it is done. If liquid runs red, bird is not done.

Cornbread Stuffing

The day before your feast, bake the Cornbread and the Biscuits for the stuffing. Store them at room temperature in plastic bags.

Cornbread:
2 eggs
2 cups buttermilk
2 cups cornmeal
3 tsp. baking powder
1 tsp. baking soda

1-1/2 tsp. salt
1-1/2 cups all-purpose flour
1 tbs. sugar
1/4 cup hot vegetable oil or bacon fat

Beat eggs and buttermilk together. Sift together the dry ingredients and add to the egg-butter-milk mixture with a few strokes. Mix until just moistened. Heat a 9 x 13-inch baking pan with oil or bacon fat for 10 minutes in a 400°F. oven. Coat pan well with fat. Pour excess fat into batter and stir until combined. Pour batter into oiled pan. Bake for 35 to 40 minutes. Cut into squares and set aside.

Biscuits:

3 cups all-purpose flour	1 tsp. baking soda
1 tsp. salt	1/2 cup shortening
4 tsp. baking powder	1-1/2 cups buttermilk

Sift the dry ingredients together and cut in the shortening. Add the buttermilk. Stir until just combined. Turn out onto a large floured board or pastry cloth. Knead 5 strokes. Roll or pat to about a 1/2-inch thickness. Cut with a biscuit cutter. Place on a well-greased baking sheet that has been preheated for 5 minutes. Bake at 450ºF. for 12 minutes, or until golden brown. Set aside for stuffing.

Stuffing:

2 cups chopped celery	2 to 4 cups chicken broth
1-1/2 cups chopped onion	2 tsp. salt
1/2 cup butter	1/2 tsp. pepper
1 recipe for Cornbread	1 tbs. sage
1 recipe for Biscuits	5 eggs

Remove the celery and onion from the refrigerator (see DAY BEFORE). Melt butter in a large skillet over medium heat. Add celery and onion. Saute for 10 to 15 minutes, stirring occasionally. Meanwhile, break cornbread and biscuits into small bits. Place in a large mixing bowl. Add sauteed celery and onions to bowl. Heat broth and add, 1/2 cup at a time, to the bread. Beat in salt, pepper and sage. The mixture should be rather fluid at this point, like a thick pudding. Beat in eggs. Taste for seasonings. Stuff neck and cavity of turkey. Put remaining stuffing in a lightly buttered baking pan. Bake for 1 hour before serving. Cook with Yams when turkey comes out of oven.

From To My Daughter With Love

Giblet Gravy

3 cups chicken broth and a cup of drippings from the turkey
6 tbs. cornstarch mixed with enough cold water to make a thin paste
1/2 cup chopped giblets (see DAY BEFORE)
1 chopped hard-boiled egg
salt and pepper to taste

Bring the chicken broth to a boil, add the cup of pan drippings to this. Lower the heat and stir in the thin cornstarch paste. Cook and stir until the gravy boils and becomes clear. Add the giblets and egg and cover. Keep on heat, but do not boil, until serving time.

From To My Daughter With Love

Fresh Cranberry Relish

Nice to share at holiday time. It makes a delightful "from-my-kitchen" gift. Pack relish in French jelly jars to within 1 inch of top. Pour a small amount of melted paraffin on relish. Top jar with a circle of brightly-colored calico. Secure with a ribbon or piece of string.

2 red-skinned apples
1 large orange
3 cups firm fresh cranberries
1-1/2 cups sugar
1/8 tsp. salt

Wash fruit. Cut apples into 6 wedges each. Remove core. Chop finely. Place in large non-metal bowl. Cut orange into quarters. Remove seeds and do not peel. Chop finely. Add to apples. Finely chop cranberries. Add to apples and oranges. Add sugar and salt. Stir well. Cover and refrigerate. Keep relish pressed below juices. A lovely red color develops as the relish stands a few days. Will keep up to one month.

Yams with Rum and Walnuts

2 lbs. yams
1-1/2 tsp. salt
1 cup dark brown sugar
1/2 cup to 2/3 cup butter
1 cup broken walnuts
2 jiggers rum

Select large red yams. Scrub and boil whole until tender. Cool and peel. Slice about 1/2-inch thick. Arrange one layer in a buttered baking dish. Sprinkle with a little salt, brown sugar and dot with plenty of butter. Add another layer of yam slices and continue as above until ingredients are used. Sprinkle walnuts on top. Pour rum over all. Bake in 350°F. oven about 30 minutes or until hot and yams have a shiny glaze. Baste occasionally during baking. More heated rum may be added during baking, if desired. Makes 12 to 16 servings.

From the Vegetable Cookbook

Green Beans Lyonnaise

3 lbs. fresh green beans
6 tbs. butter
4 large onions, thinly sliced
1 tbs. salt
1 tsp. freshly ground pepper
3 tbs. vinegar
3 tbs. freshly chopped parsley

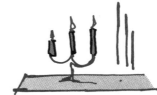

Cut ends off beans and slice into 3-inch lengths. If doing the day before, place in plastic bags in refrigerator. Melt butter in large skillet over medium heat. Add onions. Saute until lightly browned. Cool. If doing the day before, place in plastic bags in the refrigerator. Fifteen minutes before serving dish, boil beans in salted water for 10 minutes. Drain. Add onions, salt, pepper and vinegar. Taste and correct seasonings. Serve topped with parsley. Makes 12 to 16 servings.

Napkin Folding Ideas

Here are some ideas that will make your holiday table extra special.

The Swirl

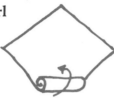   

1. Place napkin flat, with wrong side up.
    2. Beginning at corner, roll all the way up.

3. Bend in half. Place in glass.

Fifty-Fifty

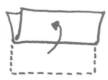 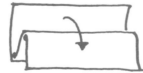

1. Place napkin right side up. Fold in half.
    2. Fold top flap down one half.

3. Turn napkin face down. Fold into quarters.

The Flapper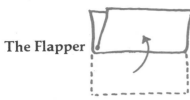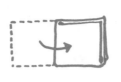

1. Place napkin right side up. Fold in half.
2. Fold in half again.   3. Fold down top flap as shown.   4. Tuck in remaining flaps.
                                    5. Fold under sides to achieve design illustrated.

The Fan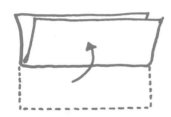

1. Fold napkin in half with right side up.
        2. By hand, or using an iron, press napkin into 1-inch accordian pleats.
            3. Place in glass. Allow pleats in top part of napkin to fall open.

Perfect Crust

A firm pastry that works well for fancy edgings and tops. If you are using only one crust, wrap the other one well and refrigerate or freeze.

9-inch, 2-crust
2 cups sifted all-purpose flour
1 tsp. salt
2/3 cup Crisco
1 egg, slightly beaten
2 tbs. cold water
2 tsp. lemon juice

Sift flour and salt into mixing bowl. Cut in shortening until particles are the size of small peas. Combine egg, water and lemon juice. Sprinkle over dry ingredients, tossing with fork until mixture is moist enough to hold together. If more water is needed, add it a few drops at a time. Form into two flat patties about 1/2-inch thick. Refrigerate at least 10 minutes (longer, if possible) before rolling.

From Pies and Cakes

Pumpkin Pie

3 eggs
1-1/2 cups evaporated milk
1-112 cups canned pumpkin
1 cup sugar
dash salt
1/2 tsp. cinnamon
2 tsp. butter
nutmeg
1 parbaked 9-inch pie shell (parbake 1/2 recipe for Perfect crust for 7 minutes at 425°F.)
sweetened whipped cream (optional)

In large mixing bowl, beat eggs and milk together well. Add pumpkin, mix well. Beat in sugar, salt and cinnamon. Continue beating until mixed thoroughly. Pour into prepared pie shell. Dot with butter and sprinkle with nutmeg. Bake at 425°F. for about 30 minutes, or until knife inserted into center of pie comes out clean. Serve with whipped cream. This pie serves 8. Make 2 pies to serve 12 to 16.

Favorite Fruitcake

At Christmas it's traditional to cut the fruitcake that has been mellowing in brandy since early in November. Make it well before Thanksgiving and store it in a lovely tin, but don't forget it. Check it often to be sure it is moist with brandy.

1/2 lb. red candied cherries
1/4 lb. green candied cherries
1 lb. mixed candied fruit
8 ozs. candied pineapple
4 ozs. golden raisins
1 lb. pecans, broken
1/2 lb. English walnuts, broken
4-1/2 cups all-purpose flour
2-1/4 cups sugar

1 cup butter
2/3 cup margarine
6 eggs, separated
2/3 cup milk
1/3 cup brandy
2 tbs. rum
1 tsp. vanilla
1 tsp. cream of tartar

Grease, line with brown paper and grease again, 3 loaf pans and 1 angel cake tube pan. In a large roasting pan, mix the candied fruit and nuts with 1 cup flour. Set aside. Cream the sugar, butter and margarine. Add the egg yolks and beat with an electric mixer at medium speed until quite creamy. Add the flour alternately with the liquids and vanilla. Beat the egg whites with the cream of tartar until very stiff. Mix the creamed mixture with the fruit and nuts. Fold in the egg whites, gently but thoroughly. Fill the prepared pans about two-thirds full, dividing the batter equally among the pans. If you wish, two tube pans may be used. The three small loaf pans are nice because they can be given as gifts. Bake at 275°F. for about 3 hours. Cool on a rack in the pans. When cool, remove from pans and drizzle with 1/4 cup brandy. Store in tightly sealed containers but check on them once a week. If all the brandy appears to have been absorbed, add another 1/4 cup of brandy in the same manner.

From To My Daughter With Love

New Year's Eve Buffet and Cocktail Party

You don't have to be a magician to throw a successful party, just organized. The following is a list of items you'll want to consider if you're planning a party:

- Have plenty of ice on hand. Make it ahead and store it in plastic bags or buy it at your local quick shop.
- If you plan to invite 15 or more people, consider hiring a bartender and a person to serve and/or clean up. That way you won't get stuck all night at the bar or in the kitchen. You'll have time to mingle more freely and make sure other aspects of your party are running smoothly.
- To promote mingling, set up the bar and the food in at least two or three different areas. This will prevent everyone from congregating in only one area of your home.
- Keep hot appetizers hot and cold appetizers cold. Use fondue pots, chaffing dishes or hot plates to keep foods hot and trays or bowls of ice to keep foods cold.
- Use fresh floral arrangements to help pull your decorating together.
- Use music to help you set the mood for the party. Records and tapes are an alternative, but they must be changed periodically. A live musician can often be hired for very little money. A high school or college pianist or guitarist is a welcome addition to any celebration.
- If parking near your home is limited, send maps with your invitations which detail

convenient parking on nearby streets.

Once you've decided upon the specifics of your party, prepare a list or "plan of action." Send out invitations as soon as possible. A month is usually sufficient notice, but during the holiday season, plans are often made several months in advance. If you are hiring any one to assist you, call them as far in advance as possible. If you are decorating your house, do as much of it as possible a day or two before your party.

It's equally important to have a timetable in mind for the food you serve. Tailor your schedule to allow advance preparation or partial preparation of as many dishes as possible. Read each recipe carefully and make sure you understand each step. Try to envision the finished product. Estimate the preparation time. Keep your cooking utensils and appliances in mind: make sure you don't have two dishes that require baking at different temperatures if you have only one oven. Make sure you have ample refrigerator space. If you don't—improvise, use an ice chest or "borrow space" in the refrigerator of a neighbor. Lastly, make a list of the cooking time of each dish you are serving. Working backwards from your scheduled serving time, decide when you should start the first dish and proceed accordingly.

Menu

Popular Drink Recipes
A Trio of Punches
Hot Meatball Appetizers
Cherry Cream Cheese Spread
Stuffed Cherry Tomatoes, Crudites with Clam and Leek Dip
Hot Stuffed Mushroom Caps
Simply Elegant Quiche
Bourbon Bread, Cookie Jewels
Peanut Butter Kisses, Chinese Almond Cookies
Serves 15 to 20

How To Make Great Drinks

Before anyone can be admitted to the bar, it is appropriate that he or she prepare to pass a bar examination. We therefore submit the following review course of ''bar basics'' to assist you.

BASIC RULES

Always use sparkling clean glassware.
Always use fresh ice
Always serve iced drinks well chilled—the colder the better
Always measure accurately. Many drinks are spoiled by being too weak or too strong.
Superfine sugar dissolves more easily than granulated
Stir clear drinks and all-liquor drinks.
Gently stir carbonated drinks.
Shake or blend drinks with fruit juices, powdered mixes, sugar, egg, cream or other ingredients difficult to mix
Add garnishes for eye appeal

From Cocktails & Hors d' Oeuvres

A Well-Stocked Bar

While the size of the bottles may vary depending on your frequency of use, a basic bar should have the following:

Blended Whiskey
Bourbon
Brandy
Gin
Light Rum
Scotch
Vodka

Vermouth, dry (French) and sweet (Italian)
Cocktail Sherry
2 to 3 favorite liqueurs
Table Wines—white, rosé and red
Beer
Soft drinks and juices for non-drinking friends

Other Ingredients and Garnishes:
Bitters
Superfine Sugar
Prepared Mixes
Mixers—club soda, tonic water, gingerale, 7-Up, collins mix, cola
Garnishes—cherries, olives, orange slices, cocktail onions

From Cocktails & Hors d'Oeuvres

Popular Drink Recipes

Bacardi Cocktail—in a shaker jar filled with ice, combine 1-1/2 ounces light rum, juice of 1/2 lime and 1/2 teaspoon grenadine. Shake well. Strain mixture into a cocktail glass.

Bloody Mary—In a glass filled with ice, pour 1 to 2 jiggers of vodka. Add 2 to 3 drops Tabasco sauce, dash of Worcestershire sauce, celery salt and pepper to taste. Fill remainder of glass with tomato juice. Stir. Garnish with a celery stalk.

Collins—Pour the juice of 1 lemon, 1 teaspoon of sugar and 2 ounces of gin into a glass filled with ice. Stir. Fill remainder of glass with club soda. Garnish with slice of orange, lemon and a cherry.

Fancy Coffees—Pour 6 ounces of fresh coffee into a mug. Add 1 teaspoon of sugar and 1 to 2 ounces of any one of the following liqueurs: Kahlua, Amaretto, Irish whiskey, brandy, creme de cacao, creme de menthe or Tia Maria.

Kir—In a large chilled wine glass, add 2 to 3 ice cubes, 1 tablespoon Creme de Cassis and 6 ounces of dry white wine. Drop a twist of lemon peel into the glass and serve.

Manhattan—Combtine 1/2 ounce sweet, Italian vermouth, 1 dash of bitters and 1-1/2 ounces of blended whiskey in a cocktail glass. Stir. Add ice. Garnish with a cherry.

Martini—Chill glass. Fill martini pitcher with cracked ice. Add 1/2 ounce gin, then 1/2 ounce dry, French vermouth. Stir briskly until well chilled. Strain into frosty glass. Garnish with an olive. To make a dry martini, increase gin to 2-1/2 ounces.

44

Margarita—Moisten cocktail glass rim with lime juice. Dip rim in salt, if desired. Shake 1 ounce fresh lime or lemon juice, 1-1/2 ounces Tequila and 1 ounce of Cointreau together with cracked ice. Strain into cocktail glass. Garnish with a thin slice of lime placed on rim of glass.

Old-Fashioned—In a glass, mix together 1/2 teaspoon sugar, 2 dashes of bitters and 1 teaspoon water or club soda until sugar is dissolved. Add 2 to 3 ice cubes and 1-1/2 ounces blended whiskey. Stir. Garnish with an orange slice and a cherry.

Piña Colada—Stir together 1 ounce cream of coconut, 2 ounces pineapple juice and 1-1/2 ounces rum. Pour into a glass filled with crushed ice. Garnish with a pineapple spear.

Screwdriver—Fill a glass with ice cubes. Add 1-1/2 ounces of vodka and fill remainder of glass with orange juice. Stir. Garnish with a pineapple spear.

Strawberry, Peach or Banana Daiquiri—Combine 16 ounces frozen strawberries or peaches (or 5 bananas) and 1/2 to 1 cup cream of coconut, 1/4 cup fresh lemon juice and 1 cup rum in a blender or food processor. Blend or process until smooth. Serves 4.

Tequila Sunrise—Pour 1-1/2 ounces Tequila and 3 ounces orange juice into a tall glass. Stir. Add ice cubes. Slowly pour in 1/2 ounce grenadine. Allow to settle. Garnish with orange slice and cherry.

Wine Spritzer—Fill a wine glass with equal parts white wine and 7-Up.

A Trio of Punches

Choose one of these luscious concoctions for your buffet table.

BOURBON PUNCH

1 fifth bourbon	1 cup pineapple juice	1/2 cup lemon juice
4 ozs. dark rum	1 cup grapefruit juice	2 quarts club soda

Have all ingredients chilled. Mix together everything, except club soda. Pour over a block of ice in a punch bowl. Just before serving, add club soda and garnish with orange slices and cherries.

CELEBRITY PUNCH

2 qts. grape juice	1 fifth gin
1 pt. orange juice	1 qt. gingerale

Combine grape juice, orange juice and gin. Pour over a block of ice in punch bowl. Just before serving add gingerale. Garnish with fruit.

FRENCH "75" PUNCH

4 bottles champagne	2 qts. club soda
2 fifths brandy	

Make an ice mold with fruit of your choice, use a ring mold. Just before serving, pour champagne, brandy and club soda over ice. Stir to mix.

From Cocktails & Hors d' Oeuvres

Meatball Appetizer

1 lb. very lean ground beef
1 tsp. Accent (optional)
salt and pepper
2 tbs. instant minced onion
1/2 cup soft breadcrumbs
1/4 cup milk
2 tbs. all-purpose flour

2 tbs. butter
3 tbs. molasses
3 tbs. prepared mustard
3 tbs. vinegar
1/4 cup catsup
1/4 tsp. thyme
wooden toothpicks

In a mixing bowl, blend meat with Accent, salt, pepper and minced onion. Use a light hand. Combine bread and milk. Add to meat. Toss lightly until well combined. Form into 3/4-inch balls.* Roll in flour. Melt butter in large skillet over medium-high heat. Add meatballs and brown. Combine remaining ingedients. Add to meatballs. Simmer over low heat about 10 minutes, or until sauce thickens, stirring occasionally. Serve hot in a chafing dish with toothpicks. Makes about 50 meatballs.

*May be frozen at this point for up to 2 months. Allow to defrost before rolling in flour and browning.

From Fast and Delicious

Cherry Cream Cheese Spread

This unusual combination will delight your guests. The flavor of most nuts is enhanced by toasting. Spread them in a single layer on a cookie sheet. Bake at 350° F. for 10 to 15 minutes, stirring occasionally until golden.

2 cups pitted Bing cherries (frozen or canned), thoroughly drained
1 cup Grand Mariner liqueur
4 pkgs. (8 ozs. each) cream cheese
2 cups chopped toasted almonds
mild-flavored crackers

Cover cherries with liqueur and refrigerate for 24 hours. Drain and discard liqueur. Beat cream cheese with an electric mixer until fluffy. By hand, stir in cherries and almonds. Using plastic wrap, shape mixture into 2 balls or logs. Wrap and store in the refrigerator.*
    *Keeps well for up to two weeks.

Stuffed Cherry Tomatoes

Cherry tomatoes seem to be a natural when it comes to appetizers. Try filling them with one of the following:

36 cherry tomatoes

Filling Suggestions:
*smoked oysters
*guacamole
*mayonnaise with cooked, crumbled bacon and chopped green chives
*cream cheese mixed with salmon, chopped chives and Worcestershire sauce

Wash and stem tomatoes. Hollow centers with a serrated knife. Turn upside down on paper towels to drain for about 15 minutes. Fill with desired filling. Chill for 15 minutes.

Crudités with Clam and Leek Dip

2 pints sour cream
2 pkgs. (2-3/4 ozs. each) dried Cream of Leek Soup Mix
2 cans (7 ozs. each) chopped, drained clams
assorted raw vegetables, such as broccoli, carrots, celery, jicama, cauliflower, cucumber,
  cut up

Mix all dip ingredients together well. Refrigerate at least 1 hour before serving. Arrange crudites attractively around dip at serving time.

From Fast and Delicious

Stuffed Mushroom Caps

Use either the Sausage or Spinach Souffle Stuffing for these tasty morsels.

30 small mushrooms, as uniform
  in size as possible
Sausage stuffing:
1 pkg. (12 ozs.) hot sausage

Spinach Souffle stuffing:
1 pkg. (12 ozs.) frozen spinach
  souffle, thawed
1/4 up grated Parmesan cheese

Wash mushrooms thoroughly under cold running water. Carefully pull off and discard stems. Dry caps with paper towels.

For Sausage stuffing: Roll sausage into small balls, each ball containing about 1 teaspoon sausage. Stuff each mushroom cap with one ball of sausage.

For Spinach Souffle stuffing: Place 1 teaspoon of thawed souffle into each mushroom cap. Sprinkle top with 1/2 teaspoon of cheese.*

Place caps 1 inch apart on ungreased cookie sheet. Bake at 350°F. for about 12 minutes. Makes 30 appetizers.

*May be made up to three days in advance.

Simply Elegant Quiche

This recipe is an adaptation of one from John McGarry, a White House chef during the Kennedy, Johnson and Nixon administrations. A delightful man with charm and good humor, he says this quiche was a favorite of Jackie Onassis and Henry Kissinger.

1/2 cup finely minced shallots
1/2 cup dry white wine
2 cups heavy cream
1 tsp. salt

1/4 tsp. white pepper
1/4 tsp. freshly grated nutmeg
6 ozs. shredded imported Gruyere cheese
1 prebaked 10-inch pie shell with a high rim

Place shallots and white wine in a small saucepan. Bring to a boil over low heat and simmer for 2 minutes. Remove and set aside to cool. Beat eggs and cream together very gently. Fold in shallot mixture and spices. Sprinkle cheese over bottom of prepared crust. Pour in custard mixture. Bake at 350°F. for 35 to 45 minutes, or until custard is set. Cover edges of pie crust with foil if crust gets too dark. Let quiche set for 10 minutes prior to serving. Serves 6 to 8. Also delicious served cold.

From Brunch

Bourbon Bread

A wonderful treat for Yuletide party guests. Wrap loaves in red or green celophane, tie with plaid ribbon and give as gifts.

4 cups unbleached all-purpose flour
5 tsp. baking powder
1 tsp. baking soda
3 tsp. mace or nutmeg
2 cups chopped pecans or walnuts

2 cups sugar
2 cups sour cream
2 eggs, well beaten
1/2 cup vegetable oil
1 cup bourbon

Preheat over to 350°F. Stir together flour, baking powder, baking soda, salt, mace, nuts and sugar. Mix sour cream, eggs, oil and bourbon together well. Add this mixture to dry ingredients. Stir until just blended. Pour into 2 buttered and floured loaf pans, each measuring 9 x 5 x 3-inches. If desired, sprinkle batter with sugar before baking. Bake for 1 hour, or until toothpick inserted into center of loaves comes out clean. Cool in pan for about 5 minutes. Turn out onto wire rack to cool completely. Makes 2 loaves. Saves well for up to a week.

Cookie Jewels

1/2 cup butter or margarine, softened
and cut into 1-inch cubes
1/4 cup light brown sugar, firmly packed
1 egg, separated
1 tsp. vanilla
1 cup all purpose flour

1/2 cup finely chopped pecans or walnuts
3 tbs. preserves (apricot or raspberry are
favorites)
1/4 cup powdered sugar
2 tsp. milk

In work bowl of food processor, or with electric mixer, cream together butter, brown sugar, egg yolk and vanilla until smooth. Add flour and process or beat until just blended. Refrigerate dough 30 minutes. Beat egg white until foamy. Roll balls of dough with the palms of your hands, to about 1 inch in diameter. Dip in foamy egg white. Roll in nuts. Place 1 inch apart on ungreased cookie sheet. With your thumb, press an indentation into the center of each cookie. Place 1/2 teaspoon of preserves into indentation. Bake at 350°F. for 8 minutes, or until lightly browned. Remove to wire rack and cool. In small bowl, combine powdered sugar and milk. Mix until lumps disappear. Drizzle cookies with glaze. Makes about 4 dozen cookies.

From Convection Oven Cookbook

Peanut Butter Kisses

1 cup butter or margarine, cut
   into 1-inch cubes
1 cup sugar
1 cup brown sugar, firmly packed
1 tbs. vanilla
2 eggs, beaten

1 cup peanut butter, creamy or chunky
3 cups all-purpose flour
2 tsp. baking soda
1/4 tsp. salt
2 pkgs. (9 ozs. each) Hershey's chocolate
   kisses, unwrapped

In work bowl of food processor, or with electric mixer, cream butter and sugars until light and fluffy. Add vanilla, eggs and peanut butter and process or beat until just blended. Remove blade from processor. By hand, stir in flour, baking soda and salt. Mix until a dough forms. Roll a tablespoon of dough in your hands until a ball forms. Place balls 2 inches apart on an ungreased cookie sheet. Bake at 350°F. for 10 minutes. As soon as cookies are done, press one chocolate kiss into the center of each cookie. Set aside to cool. Do not touch kisses until cookies have completely cooled because they will be soft. Makes 6 to 8 dozen cookies.

From Convection Oven Cookbook

Chinese Almond Cookies

Have you ever wondered what to serve for dessert after a Chinese dinner? These cookies may be your answer. The flavor the lard imparts to these cookies is essential; do not substitute butter or margarine.

1 cup lard, cut into 1-inch cubes
1 cup sugar
1 egg
1 tsp. almond extract

3 cups all-purpose flour
1 tsp. baking soda
1 tsp. salt
1 pkg. (3 ozs.) whole, blanched almonds

In work bowl of food processor, or with electric mixer, cream lard and sugar until light and fluffy. Add egg and almond extract. Process or beat until just blended. Remove blade from processor. By hand, stir in flour, baking soda and salt. Mix well. Shape dough into 1-inch balls. Place two inches apart on ungreased cookie sheet. Flatten slightly with thumb. Place 1 almond in center of each cookie. Bake at 350°F. for about 10 minutes, or until cookies are just beginning to turn golden brown. Makes 4 dozen cookies.

From Convection Oven Cookbook

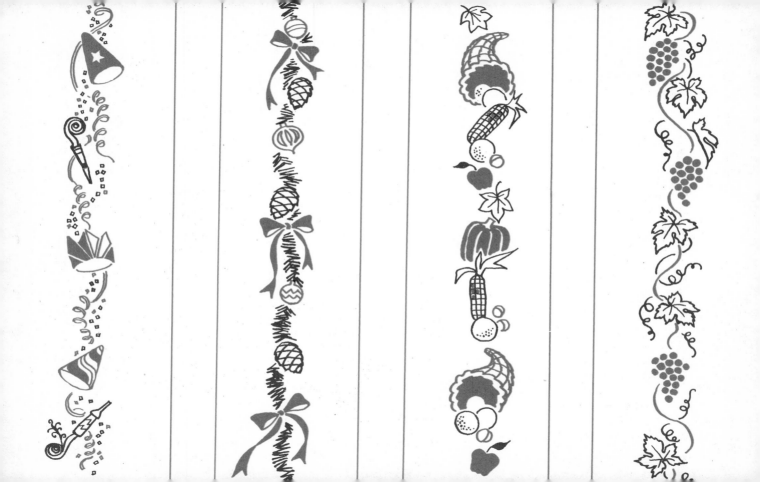

Index